21 DAYS

To a Better Way of Thinking

A 21-DAY JOURNAL TO HELP YOU BUILD YOUR LIFE ON TRUTH

DALE A. O'SHIELDS

COR
PUBLISHING

Published in Gaithersburg, Maryland, by COR Publishing
ISBN: 978-0-9984731-9-2
Learn more about the author at www.DaleOShields.com.

Every effort has been made to identify and trace copyright holders and to obtain their permission for the use of copyrighted material. The publisher apologizes for any errors or omissions and would be grateful if notified of any corrections that should be incorporated in future reprints or editions of this book.

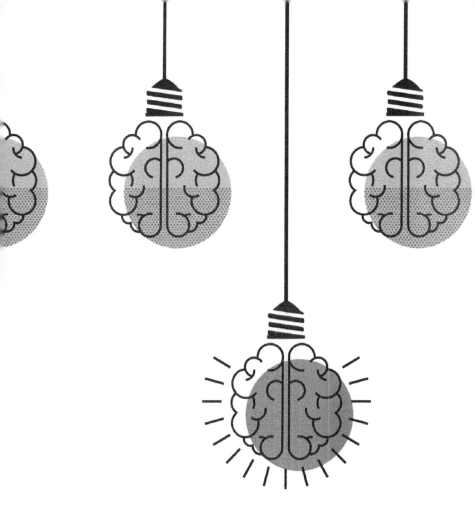

ROMANS 12:2 NLT
Don't copy the behavior and customs of this world,
but let God transform you into a new person by
changing the way you think. Then you will learn to
know God's will for you, which is good and pleasing
and perfect.

21 DAYS
TO A BETTER WAY
OF THINKING

It's a proven fact that your thinking affects your health—spiritually, emotionally, relationally, and even physically. The better your thinking, the better your life.

Many of our struggles in life come from wrong thinking—thinking based on false ideas, assumptions and perspectives. To improve our thoughts we have to build our thinking patterns on truth.

This is what this **"21 Days To a Better Way of Thinking"** journal does. It helps you build a holier, healthier and more wholesome way of thinking, based on the truth of God's Word. The goal is an improved life, more positive feelings, more loving relationships, and more productive living.

As you progress through the 21-day process you'll find the following items to focus on each day.

1. A general declaration from God's Word, validated by Scripture verses or passage. These are to be read and declared, preferably out loud to yourself.

2. A section to record what the affirmation means to you.

3. A place to record your own personal declaration focused on counteracting a specific and unique unhealthy thought pattern in your life.

4. A place to record 3 things you're thankful for. Gratitude is a key to healthier thinking.

5. A place to record at least one way you plan to serve someone each day. This helps you focus beyond yourself.

6. A place to record a special prayer.

I know this process will improve your life. Commit to it and you'll see!

Dale A. O'Shields
Senior Pastor
Church of the Redeemer

P.S. The way to a relationship with God is through His Son, Jesus Christ. If you have never invited Him into your life, do it today! Here are some Bible verses showing us how to receive Jesus Christ in your life.

ROMANS 3:23 **NIV**
For all have sinned and fall short of the glory of God.

ROMANS 5:8 **NIV**
But God demonstrates his own love for us in this: While we were still sinners, Christ died for us.

ROMANS 6:23 **NIV**
For the wages of sin is death, but the gift of God is eternal life in Christ Jesus our Lord.

ROMANS 10:9, 10, 13 **NIV**
If you declare with your mouth, "Jesus is Lord," and believe in your heart that God raised him from the dead, you will be saved. For it is with your heart that you believe and are justified, and it is with your mouth that you profess your faith and are saved...for, "Everyone who calls on the name of the Lord will be saved."

Below is a simple prayer to pray if you want a relationship with God. When you sincerely pray this prayer and put your faith in Jesus, He'll come into your life!

> *"Dear God, I admit that I have chosen my own way instead of Yours and sinned against You. I am a sinner. I'm so sorry for all my sins and turn away from them now to You. I believe that Jesus is the Son of God. I believe that He died on the cross to pay for my sins. I believe that Jesus rose from the dead. Jesus, I ask you to come into my life and take control of me. I receive you as my Lord and Savior. Thank you for forgiving me and saving me. Thank you for answering my prayer and coming into my life. In Jesus' name Amen."*

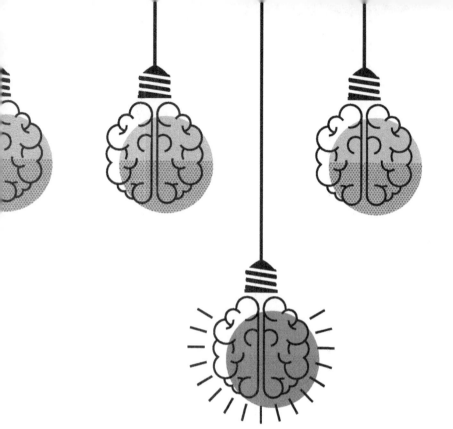

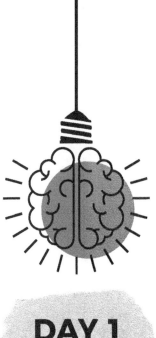

DAY 1

GOD'S WORD IS TRUE AND RELIABLE.

JOSHUA 21:45 **NLT**
Not a single one of all the good promises the LORD
had given to the family of Israel was left unfulfilled;
everything he had spoken came true.

PSALM 18:30 **NLT**
God's way is perfect. All the Lord's promises prove true.
He is a shield for all who look to him for protection.

PSALM 119:160 **TPT**
The sum total of all your words adds up to absolute truth,
and every one of your righteous decrees is everlasting.

WHAT DO THESE AFFIRMATIONS MEAN TO ME?

_____

_____

_____

_____

_____

_____

_____

_____

MY PERSONAL AFFIRMATION FOR TODAY IS...

_____

_____

_____

_____

_____

_____

_____

_____

TODAY I AM GRATEFUL FOR...

1. _____

2. _____

3. _____

I WILL SERVE OTHERS TODAY BY...

_____

_____

_____

_____

_____

_____

_____

_____

MY PRAYER FOR TODAY IS...

_____

_____

_____

_____

_____

_____

_____

_____

DAY 2

GOD IS KIND AND GOOD.

ISAIAH 54:10 **NIV**
"Though the mountains be shaken and the hills be removed,
yet my unfailing love for you will not be shaken nor my covenant
of peace be removed," says the LORD, who has compassion on you.

NAHUM 1:7 **NLT**
The LORD is good, a strong refuge when trouble comes.
He is close to those who trust in him.

PSALM 86:5 **NLT**
Lord, you are so good, so ready to forgive, so full of
unfailing love for all who ask for your help.

WHAT DO THESE AFFIRMATIONS MEAN TO ME?

_____

_____

_____

_____

_____

_____

_____

_____

MY PERSONAL AFFIRMATION FOR TODAY IS...

_____

_____

_____

_____

_____

_____

_____

_____

TODAY I AM GRATEFUL FOR...

1. _____

2. _____

3. _____

I WILL SERVE OTHERS TODAY BY...

_____

_____

_____

_____

_____

_____

_____

MY PRAYER FOR TODAY IS...

_____

_____

_____

_____

_____

_____

_____

DAY 3

GOD LOVES ME AND WANTS TO BLESS ME.

1 JOHN 3:1 **NLT**

See how very much our Father loves us, for he calls us his children, and that is what we are! But the people who belong to this world don't recognize that we are God's children because they don't know him.

ROMANS 8:38-39 **NLT**

And I am convinced that nothing can ever separate us from God's love. Neither death nor life, neither angels nor demons, neither our fears for today nor our worries about tomorrow—not even the powers of hell can separate us from God's love. No power in the sky above or in the earth below—indeed, nothing in all creation will ever be able to separate us from the love of God that is revealed in Christ Jesus our Lord.

1 CHRONICLES 4:10 **NIV**

Jabez cried out to the God of Israel, "Oh, that you would bless me and enlarge my territory! Let your hand be with me, and keep me from harm so that I will be free from pain." And God granted his request.

WHAT DO THESE AFFIRMATIONS MEAN TO ME?

_____

_____

_____

_____

_____

_____

_____

_____

_____

MY PERSONAL AFFIRMATION FOR TODAY IS...

_____

_____

_____

_____

_____

_____

_____

_____

_____

TODAY I AM GRATEFUL FOR...

1. _____

2. _____

3. _____

I WILL SERVE OTHERS TODAY BY...

_____

_____

_____

_____

_____

_____

_____

_____

MY PRAYER FOR TODAY IS...

_____

_____

_____

_____

_____

_____

_____

_____

DAY 4

GOD HAS A PURPOSE
FOR MY LIFE.

JEREMIAH 29:11 NIV
"For I know the plans I have for you," declares the Lord, "plans to prosper
you and not to harm you, plans to give you hope and a future."

EPHESIANS 2:10 GW
God has made us what we are. He has created us in Christ Jesus
to live lives filled with good works that he has prepared for us to do.

EXODUS 9:16 NLT
But I have spared you for a purpose—to show you
my power and to spread my fame throughout the earth.

WHAT DO THESE AFFIRMATIONS MEAN TO ME?

_____
_____
_____
_____
_____
_____
_____
_____
_____

MY PERSONAL AFFIRMATION FOR TODAY IS...

_____
_____
_____
_____
_____
_____
_____
_____
_____

TODAY I AM GRATEFUL FOR...

1. _____

2. _____

3. _____

I WILL SERVE OTHERS TODAY BY...

_____

_____

_____

_____

_____

_____

_____

MY PRAYER FOR TODAY IS...

_____

_____

_____

_____

_____

_____

_____

DAY 5

I AM GIFTED BY GOD.

PSALM 139:14 **NLT**
Thank you for making me so wonderfully complex!
Your workmanship is marvelous—how well I know it.

1 CORINTHIANS 12:7 **NLT**
A spiritual gift is given to each of us so we can help each other.

MATTHEW 10:29-31 **NLT**
What is the price of two sparrows—one copper coin? But not a single
sparrow can fall to the ground without your Father knowing it. And the
very hairs on your head are all numbered. So don't be afraid;
you are more valuable to God than a whole flock of sparrows.

WHAT DO THESE AFFIRMATIONS MEAN TO ME?

_____

_____

_____

_____

_____

_____

_____

_____

MY PERSONAL AFFIRMATION FOR TODAY IS...

_____

_____

_____

_____

_____

_____

_____

_____

TODAY I AM GRATEFUL FOR...

1. _____

2. _____

3. _____

I WILL SERVE OTHERS TODAY BY...

_____

_____

_____

_____

_____

_____

_____

_____

MY PRAYER FOR TODAY IS...

_____

_____

_____

_____

_____

_____

_____

_____

DAY 6

I TRUST GOD TODAY AND FOR MY FUTURE.

PSALM 28:7 **NLT**
The LORD is my strength and shield. I trust him with all my heart. He helps me, and my heart is filled with joy. I burst out in songs of thanksgiving.

HEBREWS 13:6 **NLT**
So we can say with confidence, "The LORD is my helper, so I will have no fear. What can mere people do to me?"

PSALM 20:7-8 **NIV**
Some trust in chariots and some in horses, but we trust in the name of the LORD our God. They are brought to their knees and fall, but we rise up and stand firm.

WHAT DO THESE AFFIRMATIONS MEAN TO ME?

_____

_____

_____

_____

_____

_____

_____

_____

_____

MY PERSONAL AFFIRMATION FOR TODAY IS...

_____

_____

_____

_____

_____

_____

_____

_____

_____

TODAY I AM GRATEFUL FOR...

1. _____

2. _____

3. _____

I WILL SERVE OTHERS TODAY BY...

_____

_____

_____

_____

_____

_____

_____

_____

MY PRAYER FOR TODAY IS...

_____

_____

_____

_____

_____

_____

_____

_____

DAY 7

GOD IS WORKING GOOD IN AND THROUGH MY LIFE.

ROMANS 8:28 **NLT**
And we know that God causes everything to work
together for the good of those who love God and
are called according to his purpose for them.

PHILIPPIANS 2:13 **NLT**
For God is working in you, giving you the desire
and the power to do what pleases him.

PHILIPPIANS 1:6 **NLT**
And I am certain that God, who began the good work
within you, will continue his work until it is finally
finished on the day when Christ Jesus returns.

WHAT DO THESE AFFIRMATIONS MEAN TO ME?

_____

_____

_____

_____

_____

_____

_____

_____

MY PERSONAL AFFIRMATION FOR TODAY IS...

_____

_____

_____

_____

_____

_____

_____

_____

_____

TODAY I AM GRATEFUL FOR...

1. _____
2. _____
3. _____

I WILL SERVE OTHERS TODAY BY...

_____

_____

_____

_____

_____

_____

_____

MY PRAYER FOR TODAY IS..

_____

_____

_____

_____

_____

_____

_____

DAY 8

BECAUSE OF MY RELATIONSHIP WITH GOD I AM CONFIDENT AND COURAGEOUS.

PSALM 138:3 **TPT**

At the very moment I called out to you, you answered me!
You strengthened me deep within my soul and
breathed fresh courage into me.

PSALM 23:4 **NKJV**

Yea, though I walk through the valley of the
shadow of death, I will fear no evil; For You are with
me; Your rod and Your staff, they comfort me.

1 JOHN 4:18 **NLT**

Such love has no fear, because perfect love expels all fear.
If we are afraid, it is for fear of punishment, and this
shows that we have not fully experienced his perfect love.

WHAT DO THESE AFFIRMATIONS MEAN TO ME?

_____

_____

_____

_____

_____

_____

_____

_____

_____

MY PERSONAL AFFIRMATION FOR TODAY IS...

_____

_____

_____

_____

_____

_____

_____

_____

_____

_____

TODAY I AM GRATEFUL FOR...

1. _____

2. _____

3. _____

I WILL SERVE OTHERS TODAY BY...

_____

_____

_____

_____

_____

_____

_____

_____

MY PRAYER FOR TODAY IS...

_____

_____

_____

_____

_____

_____

_____

_____

DAY 9

GOD WILL SUPPLY ALL MY NEEDS.

PHILIPPIANS 4:19 **NIV**
And my God will meet all your needs according
to the riches of his glory in Christ Jesus.

MATTHEW 6:33 **NIV**
But seek first his kingdom and his righteousness, and
all these things will be given to you as well.

2 CORINTHIANS 9:8 **NLT**
And God will generously provide all you need.
Then you will always have everything you need
and plenty left over to share with others.

WHAT DO THESE AFFIRMATIONS MEAN TO ME?

_____

_____

_____

_____

_____

_____

_____

_____

_____

MY PERSONAL AFFIRMATION FOR TODAY IS...

_____

_____

_____

_____

_____

_____

_____

_____

_____

TODAY I AM GRATEFUL FOR...

1. _____

2. _____

3. _____

I WILL SERVE OTHERS TODAY BY...

_____

_____

_____

_____

_____

_____

_____

_____

MY PRAYER FOR TODAY IS...

_____

_____

_____

_____

_____

_____

_____

_____

DAY 10

I CAN BE ALL GOD CALLS ME TO BE, AND DO ALL GOD CALLS ME TO DO.

2 TIMOTHY 1:7 **NLT**
For God has not given us a spirit of fear
and timidity, but of power, love, and self-discipline.

PHILIPPIANS 4:13 **NLT**
For I can do everything through Christ, who gives me strength.

EPHESIANS 3:20 **TPT**
Never doubt God's mighty power to work in you and accomplish all
this. He will achieve infinitely more than your greatest request, your
most unbelievable dream, and exceed your wildest imagination!
He will outdo them all, for his miraculous power constantly energizes you.

WHAT DO THESE AFFIRMATIONS MEAN TO ME?

_____

_____

_____

_____

_____

_____

_____

_____

_____

MY PERSONAL AFFIRMATION FOR TODAY IS...

_____

_____

_____

_____

_____

_____

_____

_____

_____

TODAY I AM GRATEFUL FOR...

1. _____

2. _____

3. _____

I WILL SERVE OTHERS TODAY BY...

_____

_____

_____

_____

_____

_____

_____

MY PRAYER FOR TODAY IS...

_____

_____

_____

_____

_____

_____

_____

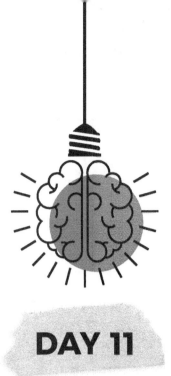

DAY 11

BECAUSE OF GOD'S BLESSINGS IN MY LIFE I AM A CHEERFUL GIVER.

LUKE 6:38 **NIV**

Give, and it will be given to you. A good measure, pressed down,
shaken together and running over, will be poured into your lap.
For with the measure you use, it will be measured to you.

PSALM 23:1 **NIV**

The LORD is my shepherd, I lack nothing.

2 CORINTHIANS 9:6 **NLT**

Remember this—a farmer who plants only a few seeds will get a small
crop. But the one who plants generously will get a generous crop.

WHAT DO THESE AFFIRMATIONS MEAN TO ME?

_____

_____

_____

_____

_____

_____

_____

_____

_____

MY PERSONAL AFFIRMATION FOR TODAY IS...

_____

_____

_____

_____

_____

_____

_____

_____

_____

TODAY I AM GRATEFUL FOR...

1. _____

2. _____

3. _____

I WILL SERVE OTHERS TODAY BY...

_____

_____

_____

_____

_____

_____

_____

_____

MY PRAYER FOR TODAY IS...

_____

_____

_____

_____

_____

_____

_____

_____

DAY 12

BECAUSE OF GOD'S FORGIVENESS I AM FREE OF THE GUILT AND SHAME OF MY PAST.

1 JOHN 1:9 **NIV**

If we confess our sins, he is faithful and just and will forgive us our sins and purify us from all unrighteousness.

ROMANS 8:1 **NLT**

So now there is no condemnation for those who belong to Christ Jesus.

LUKE 7:48 **NLT**

Then Jesus said to the woman, "Your sins are forgiven."

WHAT DO THESE AFFIRMATIONS MEAN TO ME?

_____

_____

_____

_____

_____

_____

_____

_____

_____

_____

MY PERSONAL AFFIRMATION FOR TODAY IS...

_____

_____

_____

_____

_____

_____

_____

_____

_____

_____

TODAY I AM GRATEFUL FOR...

1. _____

2. _____

3. _____

I WILL SERVE OTHERS TODAY BY...

_____

_____

_____

_____

_____

_____

_____

_____

MY PRAYER FOR TODAY IS...

_____

_____

_____

_____

_____

_____

_____

_____

_____

DAY 13

BECAUSE GOD LOVES ME
I LOVE OTHERS.

1 JOHN 4:7-8 **NLT**

Dear friends, let us continue to love one another, for love comes from God.
Anyone who loves is a child of God and knows God. But anyone who
does not love does not know God, for God is love.

1 CORINTHIANS 13:13 **NLT**

Three things will last forever—faith, hope,
and love—and the greatest of these is love.

EPHESIANS 4:32 **NLT**

Instead, be kind to each other, tenderhearted, forgiving
one another, just as God through Christ has forgiven you.

WHAT DO THESE AFFIRMATIONS MEAN TO ME?

_____

_____

_____

_____

_____

_____

_____

_____

_____

MY PERSONAL AFFIRMATION FOR TODAY IS...

_____

_____

_____

_____

_____

_____

_____

_____

_____

TODAY I AM GRATEFUL FOR...

1. _____

2. _____

3. _____

I WILL SERVE OTHERS TODAY BY...

_____

_____

_____

_____

_____

_____

_____

_____

MY PRAYER FOR TODAY IS...

_____

_____

_____

_____

_____

_____

_____

DAY 14

I SERVE OTHERS JOYFULLY.

COLOSSIANS 3:23 **TPT**
Put your heart and soul into every activity you do, as though you are doing it for the Lord himself and not merely for others.

MATTHEW 23:11 **TPT**
The greatest among you will be the one who always serves others.

PROVERBS 11:25 **NLT**
The generous will prosper; those who refresh others will themselves be refreshed.

WHAT DO THESE AFFIRMATIONS MEAN TO ME?

_____

_____

_____

_____

_____

_____

_____

_____

_____

MY PERSONAL AFFIRMATION FOR TODAY IS...

_____

_____

_____

_____

_____

_____

_____

_____

_____

TODAY I AM GRATEFUL FOR...

1. _____

2. _____

3. _____

I WILL SERVE OTHERS TODAY BY...

_____

_____

_____

_____

_____

_____

_____

_____

MY PRAYER FOR TODAY IS...

_____

_____

_____

_____

_____

_____

_____

_____

DAY 15

I EXPECT GOOD, NOT EVIL.

PSALM 23:6 NIV
Surely your goodness and love will follow me all the days of
my life, and I will dwell in the house of the Lord forever.

PROVERBS 23:18 TPT
Your future is bright and filled with a living hope that will never fade away.

ISAIAH 41:10 NLT
Don't be afraid, for I am with you. Don't be discouraged,
for I am your God. I will strengthen you and help you.
I will hold you up with my victorious right hand.

WHAT DO THESE AFFIRMATIONS MEAN TO ME?

_____

_____

_____

_____

_____

_____

_____

_____

_____

MY PERSONAL AFFIRMATION FOR TODAY IS...

_____

_____

_____

_____

_____

_____

_____

_____

_____

TODAY I AM GRATEFUL FOR...

1. _____
2. _____
3. _____

I WILL SERVE OTHERS TODAY BY...

_____

_____

_____

_____

_____

_____

_____

_____

MY PRAYER FOR TODAY IS...

_____

_____

_____

_____

_____

_____

_____

_____

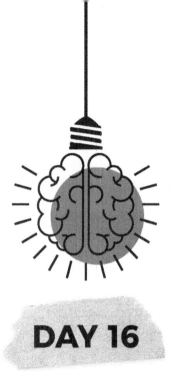

DAY 16

I OVERCOME EVIL WITH GOOD.

ROMANS 12:21 **NLT**
Don't let evil conquer you, but conquer evil by doing good.

EPHESIANS 6:12 **TLB**
For we are not fighting against people made of flesh and blood, but against persons without bodies—the evil rulers of the unseen world, those mighty satanic beings and great evil princes of darkness who rule this world; and against huge numbers of wicked spirits in the spirit world.

PROVERBS 16:7 **GW**
When a person's ways are pleasing to the Lord, he makes even his enemies to be at peace with him.

WHAT DO THESE AFFIRMATIONS MEAN TO ME?

_____

_____

_____

_____

_____

_____

_____

_____

_____

MY PERSONAL AFFIRMATION FOR TODAY IS...

_____

_____

_____

_____

_____

_____

_____

_____

_____

TODAY I AM GRATEFUL FOR...

1. _____

2. _____

3. _____

I WILL SERVE OTHERS TODAY BY...

_____

_____

_____

_____

_____

_____

_____

_____

MY PRAYER FOR TODAY IS...

_____

_____

_____

_____

_____

_____

_____

_____

DAY 17

GOD'S PEACE GUARDS MY HEART.

PHILIPPIANS 4:6-7 **TLB**

Don't worry about anything; instead, pray about everything; tell God your needs, and don't forget to thank him for his answers. If you do this, you will experience God's peace, which is far more wonderful than the human mind can understand. His peace will keep your thoughts and your hearts quiet and at rest as you trust in Christ Jesus.

ISAIAH 26:3 **NLT**

You will keep in perfect peace all who trust in you, all whose thoughts are fixed on you!

PSALM 119:165 **NLT**

Those who love your instructions have great peace and do not stumble.

WHAT DO THESE AFFIRMATIONS MEAN TO ME?

_____

_____

_____

_____

_____

_____

_____

_____

_____

MY PERSONAL AFFIRMATION FOR TODAY IS...

_____

_____

_____

_____

_____

_____

_____

_____

_____

TODAY I AM GRATEFUL FOR...

1. _____
2. _____
3. _____

I WILL SERVE OTHERS TODAY BY...

_____

_____

_____

_____

_____

_____

_____

_____

MY PRAYER FOR TODAY IS...

_____

_____

_____

_____

_____

_____

_____

_____

_____

DAY 18

GOD IS MY CONSTANT COMPANION AND FRIEND.

JOSHUA 1:9 **NLT**

This is my command—be strong and courageous! Do not be afraid or discouraged. For the LORD your God is with you wherever you go.

JOHN 15:15 **NIV**

I no longer call you servants, because a servant does not know his master's business. Instead, I have called you friends, for everything that I learned from my Father I have made known to you.

HEBREWS 13:15 **NIV**

Through Jesus, therefore, let us continually offer to God a sacrifice of praise—the fruit of lips that openly profess his name.

WHAT DO THESE AFFIRMATIONS MEAN TO ME?

_____

_____

_____

_____

_____

_____

_____

_____

MY PERSONAL AFFIRMATION FOR TODAY IS...

_____

_____

_____

_____

_____

_____

_____

_____

_____

TODAY I AM GRATEFUL FOR...

1. _____

2. _____

3. _____

I WILL SERVE OTHERS TODAY BY...

_____

_____

_____

_____

_____

_____

_____

_____

MY PRAYER FOR TODAY IS...

_____

_____

_____

_____

_____

_____

_____

_____

DAY 19

MY WEAKNESSES ARE OPPORTUNITIES TO RECEIVE GOD'S STRENGTH.

2 CORINTHIANS 12:9 **NLT**
Each time he said, "My grace is all you need. My power works best in weakness." So now I am glad to boast about my weaknesses, so that the power of Christ can work through me.

MATTHEW 12:20 **NLT**
He will not crush the weakest reed or put out a flickering candle. Finally he will cause justice to be victorious.

ISAIAH 40:29 **NLT**
He gives power to the weak and strength to the powerless.

WHAT DO THESE AFFIRMATIONS MEAN TO ME?

_____

_____

_____

_____

_____

_____

_____

_____

MY PERSONAL AFFIRMATION FOR TODAY IS...

_____

_____

_____

_____

_____

_____

_____

_____

TODAY I AM GRATEFUL FOR...

1. _____

2. _____

3. _____

I WILL SERVE OTHERS TODAY BY...

_____

_____

_____

_____

_____

_____

_____

_____

MY PRAYER FOR TODAY IS...

_____

_____

_____

_____

_____

_____

_____

_____

DAY 20

GOD HEARS AND
ANSWERS MY PRAYERS.

MATTHEW 7:7-8 **NIV**
Ask and it will be given to you; seek and you will find; knock and the door will be opened to you. For everyone who asks receives; the one who seeks finds; and to the one who knocks, the door will be opened.

PSALM 91:15 **NLT**
When they call on me, I will answer; I will be with them
in trouble. I will rescue and honor them.

HEBREWS 4:16 **NLT**
So let us come boldly to the throne of our gracious God.
There we will receive his mercy, and we will find grace
to help us when we need it most.

WHAT DO THESE AFFIRMATIONS MEAN TO ME?

_____

_____

_____

_____

_____

_____

_____

_____

_____

MY PERSONAL AFFIRMATION FOR TODAY IS...

_____

_____

_____

_____

_____

_____

_____

_____

_____

TODAY I AM GRATEFUL FOR...

1. _____
2. _____
3. _____

I WILL SERVE OTHERS TODAY BY...

_____

_____

_____

_____

_____

_____

_____

_____

MY PRAYER FOR TODAY IS...

_____

_____

_____

_____

_____

_____

_____

_____

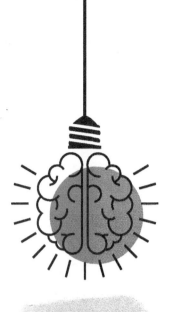

DAY 21

I LOVE GOD AND LIVE TO PLEASE HIM.

2 CORINTHIANS 5:9 NLT
So whether we are here in this body or away
from this body, our goal is to please him.

PSALM 91:14 NIV
Because he loves me," says the LORD, "I will rescue him;
I will protect him, for he acknowledges my name.

PSALM 40:8 NLT
I take joy in doing your will, my God, for
your instructions are written on my heart.

WHAT DO THESE AFFIRMATIONS MEAN TO ME?

_____

_____

_____

_____

_____

_____

_____

_____

_____

MY PERSONAL AFFIRMATION FOR TODAY IS...

_____

_____

_____

_____

_____

_____

_____

_____

_____

_____

TODAY I AM GRATEFUL FOR...

1. _____

2. _____

3. _____

I WILL SERVE OTHERS TODAY BY...

_____

_____

_____

_____

_____

_____

_____

MY PRAYER FOR TODAY IS...

_____

_____

_____

_____

_____

_____

_____

_____

ABOUT THE AUTHOR

Dale A. O'Shields is the founding and senior pastor of Church of the Redeemer, a multi-cultural and multi-generational church in the greater Washington, D.C. area.

Pastor Dale is passionate about inspiring people to grow in Christ and impact their church and community. His practical teaching makes the Bible understandable and applicable in everyday life. His messages are broadcast widely, and he has written several books and devotional resources.

In over thirty years of ministry, Pastor Dale has trained and equipped pastors and church leaders, nationally and internationally, to plant and develop strong and thriving ministries.

He and his wife Terry have two married daughters and seven grandchildren.

To know more about the author visit: www.daleoshields.com

@daleoshields

@daleoshields